IGNAT

MW01267638

Study Guide for
The Confessions
— *by Saint Augustine of Hippo* —

Edited by

Eleanor Bourg Nicholson
Joseph Pearce

Introduction by

Patrick S. J. Carmack

IGNATIUS PRESS   SAN FRANCISCO

Cover design by John Herreid

ISBN 978-1-58617-686-0

Printed in the United States of America ∞

Table of Contents

Why a Great Books Study Guide? 5

How to Use This Guide 11

Context 13

Bare Bones: The Skeleton Plot 17

**Words Made Flesh: Summary of Critical Appraisals
and Study Questions** 25

    David Vincent Meconi, S.J.:
Introduction to the *Confessions* 25

    Allan Fitzgerald, O.S.A.:
"Confession, Prayer, Transformation" 26

    Joseph T. Lienhard, S.J.: "The *Confessions*:
Augustine's First Treatise on Grace" 27

    Jared Ortiz: "Creation in the *Confessions*" 29

    Christopher J. Thompson: "Augustine's *Confessions*
and the Source of Christian Character 30

Things to Think About While Reading the Book 33

Study Questions on the Text of the *Confessions* 37

    Part One—Knowledge of the Text 37

    Part Two—Essay Questions 38

Answer Key for the *Confessions* 41

Why a Great Books Study Guide?

Wisdom is generally acknowledged to be the highest good of the human mind, whether this be recognized as knowledge of first principles and causes or as a contemplative gaze at Wisdom itself. But how does one obtain wisdom? The means is primarily conversation with great and wise persons who have already advanced far along the paths of knowledge and understanding to wisdom. As the philosopher Dr. Peter Redpath succinctly puts it when addressing audiences of young people interested in understanding why they ought to read great books, "If you wish to become wise, learn from wise people."

Since, however, persons of great wisdom are rare and generally unavailable to us due to distance or death, we enter into conversation with them through their books which record their thought. In doing this, we soon discover how all the authors of great books used this same method of study themselves. They began by conversing with or reading the great books written by the sages of earlier generations. In so doing, they avoided having to re-invent the wheel each generation; and they avoided making mistakes already dealt with and were able to build on existing foundations. Indeed what would be the point in studying mediocre works by lesser luminaries or beginning all thought over from square one every few years, when great books by the wisest people—the great sages of civilization—are readily available?

> The reading of all good books is indeed like a conversation with the noblest men of past centuries who were the authors of them, nay a carefully studied conversation, in which they reveal to us none but the best of their thoughts. (Rene Descartes, *Discourse on Method*)

Through the internal dialectical process found in the great books—
the references, discussions, critiques, and responses to the thought
of the authors' wise predecessors, a process referred to as the "Great
Conversation" by Robert M. Hutchins—we may closely follow
the development of the investigations conducted by these wise
men into the great ideas they have pondered and about which they
have written. This manner of study has always been the normative
approach to wisdom in the West.

> Until lately the West has regarded it as self-evident that the road
> to education lay through great books. No man was educated until
> he was acquainted with the masterpieces of his tradition. . . . They
> were the principal instruments of liberal education. . . . The goal
> toward which Western society moves is the Civilization of the
> Dialogue. The spirit of Western civilization is the spirit of inquiry.
> Its dominant element is *Logos*.[1]

No ongoing dialogue comparable in duration or breadth exists in
the East. Pope Benedict XVI has mentioned that Western civilization has become the dominant civilization because of its closer
correspondence to human nature. In his 2006 Regensburg lecture,
he noted that there exists a real analogy between our created reason
and God, who is *Logos* (meaning both "reason" and "word"). To
abandon reason—and hence the dialogue, which is both reason's
natural expression and necessary aid—would be contrary both to
the nature of man and of God. This cumulative wisdom of the
West is preserved and transmitted in its great music and art, but
most particularly in the study of its great books which record the
results of three millennia of dialogue, guided by reason, concerning the most profound ideas with which we must all grapple such
as existence, life, love, happiness, and so forth.

---

[1] Robert M. Hutchins, *The Great Conversation: The Substance of a Liberal Education*,
vol. 1, *The Great Books of the Western World* (Chicago: Encyclopedia Britannica, Inc.,
1952).

This manner of learning is greatly facilitated when the reader also engages in a dialectic exchange—a live conversation (in person or now online)—with other readers of the same books, probing and discussing the great ideas contained in them and, one hopes, carrying them a few steps further. This method of learning is often referred to as the Socratic method, after the ancient Athenian philosopher Socrates, who initiated its use as a deliberate way to obtain understanding and wisdom through mutual inquiry and discussion. This same "questioning" method was used by Christ, who often answered questions with other questions, parables, and stories that left the hearers wondering, questioning, and thinking. He already knew the answers, as Socrates often did. The goal was not merely indoctrination of the memory with information, facts, and knowledge, but mind- and life-changing understanding and wisdom.

This study guide is intended for students (if one is still learning, one is a student) who have read—extensively—lesser works, particularly the classic children's literature. Given that degree of preparation, students of high school age and older, including adults, can pick up Homer's *Iliad* and *Odyssey* or Herodotus' *Histories* and other great works and enter into the seminal thought of the most influential books of our culture and civilization. There is reason not to delay such education.

The great books are, for the most part, the most interesting and well written of all books. They were not written for experts. Their wide and enduring appeal to generation after generation testifies to that fact. Readers reasonably prepared for them will find them captivating, entertaining, and enlightening. Naturally, some readers will profit more than others from the great books, but all will profit from learning about the Trojan War, ancient civilizations, the heroes of ancient Greece, the early tragedies, and the thought of Aristotle. Works such as Genesis, the *Aeneid*, Saint Augustine's *Confessions*, Chaucer's *Canterbury Tales*, Dante's *Divine Comedy*, Saint Thomas Aquinas' *Summa theologica*, and Shakespeare's plays are foundational for and/or profoundly influential on our way of life. These works are essential for participation in the Great Conversation mentioned above. The enduring intellectual dialogue begins with the works of Homer, the "father of civilization", and proceeds through the centuries, eventually absorbing the Old and New Testaments in a lengthy reformulation of classical civilization into Western civilization, which continues—albeit always under assault by various errors—right up to our time.

The principal guides in selecting the works of enduring appeal to be included in the corpus of great books, besides generations of readers, include the late, great Dr. Mortimer J. Adler, who worked for eighty years (from 1921 to 2000, when I had the privilege to participate in his last Socratic discussion groups) to restore and keep the great classics, including particularly those by Plato, Aristotle, and Aquinas, in the Western canon of great books. As Dr. Adler put it, "The great books constitute the backbone of a liberal education." But read alone in our postmodernist context of radical skepticism, the great books can easily be misunderstood and used for all manner of mischief. It was precisely a desire to provide a deeper understanding of the importance and influence of the great books—to highlight what is true and great in them and to expose and defang what is false—that inspired Ignatius Press to initiate its important Critical Editions series.

Augmenting the work of Dr. Adler, on behalf of Ignatius Press, is Joseph Pearce, the author of several critically acclaimed, best-selling biographies of great authors, who has diligently worked as the author and/or editor of these study guides to accompany the Ignatius Critical Editions, of which he is also the series editor. Our gratitude extends to Father Joseph Fessio for his encouragement of this much-needed project, which is so broad in scope and vision as to be potentially revolutionary in the schools, colleges, and universities dominated by relativism. Homeschoolers, though somewhat shielded from the relativism of the schools, will find in these guides a welcome and trustworthy means of introduction to the great books and to their careful and critical reading.

Finally, it is worth emphasizing that these Ignatius Critical Editions Study Guides are merely introductory guides with tests, questions, and answer keys helpful for student assessment. The great books themselves are the primary texts, their authors our primary teachers.

Patrick S. J. Carmack
January 18, 2008

Patrick S. J. Carmack, J.D., is the president of the Great Books Academy Homeschool Program (greatbooksacademy.org), the Angelicum Academy Homeschool Program (angelicum.net), the Western Civilization Foundation, and the online publication *Classical Homeschooling Magazine* (classicalhomeschooling.com).

How to Use This Guide

The Ignatius Critical Editions (ICE) Study Guides are intended to assist students and teachers in their reading of the Ignatius Critical Editions. Each guide gives a short introductory appraisal of the contextual factors surrounding the writing of the literary work, a short "bare bones" summary of the plot, and a more in-depth summary of some of the essential critical aspects of the work. There is also a list of things to think about while reading the book, designed to focus the reader's critical faculties. These points to ponder will enable the reader to rise above a merely recreational reading of the text to a level of critical and literary appreciation befitting the work itself.

Finally, there are questions for the student to answer. These fall into two distinct categories: questions concerned with a knowledge of the *facts* of the work, and questions concerned with analyzing the *truths* that emerge from the work. This approach is rooted in the fundamental axiom, taught by great philosophers such as Aristotle and Saint Thomas Aquinas, that we must go *through* the facts *to* the truth. Put simply, an inadequate knowledge of the facts of a work (who did what and when, who said what to whom, etc.) will inevitably lead to a failure to understand the work on its deeper levels of meaning.

As such, readers of the work are strongly encouraged to answer all the *fact-related* questions in part 1. The close reading of the text that this will entail will prepare them for the essay questions in part 2. With regard to the latter, it is left to the discretion of the teacher (or the reader) as to how many of these questions should be answered. Some of the questions, particularly those calling for a contextual reading of the work in relation to other works, might be unsuitable for less-advanced students or readers. In such cases, the teacher (or reader) should use his discretion in deciding which of the essay questions should be answered. In any event, you have been provided with an abundance of questions from which to choose!

Teachers should also be aware that the answer key can be removed before the study guide is made available to the student. Answers to the questions in the "Bare Bones" and "Things to Think About" sections are not included in the answer key because these questions are intended to raise issues for the student to ponder and are not intended to be employed for examination purposes.

It should be noted that the Ignatius Critical Editions and the ICE Study Guides approach these great works of literature from a tradition-oriented perspective. Those seeking deconstruction, "queer theory", feminism, postcolonialism, and other manifestations of the latest academic fads and fashions will be disappointed. If you are unable to think outside the postmodern box, this guide is not for you!

Context

The immorality of the early life of Aurelius Augustinus (354–430), later canonized and revered by Catholics for centuries as Saint Augustine, is notorious. Augustine was born in Thagaste, Numidia (modern-day Algeria), to a pagan father, Patricius, and a devoutly Catholic mother, Monica. Monica's piety was effectively counterbalanced by Patricius' staunch paganism, and Augustine's early education reflected the division between his parents. Augustine was educated at Thagaste before being sent (through the assistance of a wealthy patron) to Carthage to study rhetoric. While in Carthage, he embraced a non-Christian lifestyle, taking a mistress (who later bore him a son named Adeodates, which means "given by God") and becoming a follower of the increasingly influential dualist religion of Manichaeism.

Manichaeism, founded toward the end of the third century, claimed to synthesize all established religions at that time. This religion, uniting Zoroastrianism, Gnosticism, Buddhism, and elements of Babylonian lore, adopted certain superficial elements from Christianity as well. Because of this, fourth-century Christianity was deeply embattled by Manichaeist influences both from within and from without. The central tenets of Manichaeism were based on the radical dualistic premise that the universe was divided between the equally powerful principles of good and evil. The religion celebrated the mind as intrinsically good, while the body was intrinsically bad. Thus it celebrated asceticism as the primary means for union with God.

In the mid-370s, Augustine continued his work as a teacher in Thagaste (briefly), as well as in both Carthage and Rome, before going on to serve as a teacher of rhetoric in Milan. It was during this time that he came into close contact with Ambrose, the bishop of Milan, and intellectually encountered the thought of the Neoplatonists. These two critical forces served to facilitate Augustine's break with his sinful lifestyle and with Manichaeism: Neoplatonism shook his already weakened trust in Manichaeist doctrines, whereas Christianity (reasonably presented by Ambrose) went further in answering all of the pressing questions that had burdened Augustine for many years. At the Easter Vigil of 387, Augustine received Christian baptism. He abandoned his work as a teacher and returned to Thagaste. In 391 he received priestly ordination and for a time served as auxiliary to Valerius, bishop of Hippo. Upon the death of Valerius in 396, Augustine was named his successor and served as bishop of Hippo until his own death in 430. Throughout these thirty years of episcopal service, Augustine continued to battle directly against the most prevalent heresies of the day, including Manichaeism, Donatism, and Pelagianism. In 1298 Pope Boniface VIII named Augustine a doctor of the Church. He is popularly now known as the Doctor of Grace because of his singular contribution to the theological understanding of divine grace.

The significance of so much biographical detail to understanding the *Confessions* is not simply attributable to the fact that it is an autobiography. In fact, though the *Confessions* is often considered one of the earliest Western specimens of the autobiographical genre (if not the earliest), the contextual situating of the *Confessions* within the framework of Augustine's life reflects elements of the work's wider relevance. Various pagan philosophers had at various times dabbled in confession-like narratives, chronicling the journey of a mind toward a given school of thought, and many Christian spiritual writers would directly follow Augustine's example in recording their gradual growth in understanding and intimacy with Christ. Augustine himself wrote the *Confessions* in part as a response to those who questioned the legitimacy of his conversion and the prudence of his elevation to the episcopacy of Hippo—he wrote the *Confessions* within two years of being named bishop.

Further, however, the narrative of his development of thought serves as the template upon which Augustine builds an elaborate and sophisticated theological structure. His personal exploration of so many of the critical heresies of his own day particularly equipped him in combatting them, and the intricacy of his faith and theological understanding united with that personal experience to give the *Confessions* a doubly lasting significance: first, in critically exploring the elements of each heresy (many of which are discernible at least in some form over a millennium and a half later), and second, and more importantly, in revealing the Truth of the trinitarian God who outlasts all error and who is personally and intimately relevant to each and every human soul. Thus the *Confessions* is appropriately attributable to a doctor of the Church ("doctor" being a title that reflects the enduring theological relevance of thought beyond the life of the thinker) and, while it is indeed the autobiographical account of Augustine's early life, can at the same time truly be described as the story of Everyman.

Bare Bones: The Skeleton Plot

"Great are you, O Lord," declares the opening line of the *Confessions*, "and exceedingly worthy of praise." This uncharacteristic beginning lays the groundwork for Saint Augustine's spiritual autobiography. The entirety of the work is thus arranged as a dialogue with God, and while it in large part chronicles the personal experiences of Augustine, it at the same time functions as the narrative of Everyman in his relationship with God: "[Y]ou have made us", continues Augustine, "and drawn us to yourself, and our heart is unquiet until it rests in you." Thus, praising God and acknowledging man's enduring need for him, Augustine opens vital questions regarding the nature of God, how man can seek him, and how to understand the relationship between the Creator and his creation. Augustine thereby situates his own life in the context of God's active presence and makes possible a simultaneous confession of faith, praise, and personal sin. The first nine books of his work will chronicle his passage from childhood ignorance, through immorality and philosophical error, to a submissive acceptance and an embrace of God. The last four books of the *Confessions* open up to a discursive exploration of God, drawing on the themes that are clearly identified through Augustine's autobiographical search.

From his prayerful and contextualizing opening, Augustine goes on in Book I to describe his infancy and childhood. He introduces many important themes that he will continue to address throughout the *Confessions*: gratitude to God for God's abundant blessings (particularly in the form of Augustine's parents); the effects of original sin (here seen even in human infancy); and the vital nature of language (both in the facilitation of formal education and in its ability to make possible communication and interaction with the divine Word). He displays a deep sensitivity in acknowledging the sins of childhood, recognizing each and every one as a building block for the formation of evil habits, culminating in the sins of adulthood. The book concludes with a prayer of gratitude.

Book II chronicles the depravity of Augustine's adolescence, particularly in the form of his burgeoning sexual desires. After studying in Madura (modern-day M'Daourouch, Algeria), he returns home to spend most of 369–370 in wanton idleness. It is during this time that he and a group of friends steal pears from a neighbor's orchard. "I plucked them only for the sake of stealing", he confesses (see *Conf.* II.6.12). He incorporates three important themes in this theft of fruit: (1) the fruit consumed from the Tree of Knowledge of Good and Evil in the Garden of Eden; (2) the prodigal son's feeding of the swine; and (3) Manichaean symbolism connected with fruit. In this admission of willful and deliberate sin, Augustine's understanding of both good and evil in the context of divine grace begins to bloom.

The next three books, spanning Augustine's life from 371 to around 386, describe his struggles as a young man through education and into his chosen profession. In 371, supported by the patronage of a wealthy family friend, Augustine travels to Carthage and begins a three-year study of rhetoric. It is during this time (described in Book III) that he plunges fully into a life of dissipation and fathers a son named Adeodatus. Augustine encounters the writings of the philosopher Cicero (particularly his *Hortensius*), which inspire Augustine to take up philosophical inquiry and a search for God. He returns briefly to the Bible but finds it insipid in comparison to the philosophical writings he has experienced and unsatisfying with regard to his own enduring questions. He then encounters and embraces Manichaeism, a Gnostic religious sect. Manichaeism, founded by a Persian mystic named Mani in the latter half of the third century, relies upon a notion of cosmic dualism whereby all of reality is attributable to an eternal battle between a good god and an equally powerful malicious god. Manichaeism thus seamlessly answers the question why evil exists and excuses Augustine's sinful behavior as an inescapable part of human reality.

In Book IV, Augustine describes his work as a teacher and denigrates himself as a "seducer" rather than an educator of those beneath him (see *Conf.* IV.1.1). He confesses his fifteen-year relationship to a common-law wife and his brief experimentation with astrology. Further, he describes the death of a close friend whom he personally led astray from Christianity to Manichaeism. Devastated by grief and confused by his friend's deathbed baptism, Augustine leaves Thagaste (where he has taught for two years) and returns to Carthage to teach. He writes his first books and reads Aristotle's *Ten Categories*.

By Book V, Augustine is increasingly disillusioned with Manichaeism, struggling with a number of nagging questions. After nine years as a Manichaean "hearer", he is finally driven from its beliefs by the ignorance of its leaders (particularly a bishop named Faustus, renowned for his learning). Augustine then leaves Carthage and goes to Rome to teach. While there, he continues his exploration for truth, still retaining elements of Manichaean belief, particularly dualism and the rejection of the Incarnation. In the autumn of 384, frustration with his students drives him from Rome to Milan. Milan is at this time the heart of the Roman Empire. Augustine reaches the pinnacle of his secular career: he becomes the imperially appointed professor of rhetoric. While in Milan, Augustine first meets Bishop Ambrose. Ambrose reveals to the searcher that both Catholicism and the Bible are philosophically defensible, in spite of Manichaean arguments to the contrary. Augustine becomes a Christian catechumenate, though he does not yet fully embrace the Truth contained within Church teaching.

In Book VI, Augustine's progress toward the Catholic faith continues. He speaks of his mother, with her unceasing faith, prayers, and example of unquestioning obedience. Further,

Augustine describes Ambrose's efforts in answering all of his most pressing questions. He considers the case of Alypius, one of his students and a close friend, who, through God's grace, endeavors to abandon his own life of sin. Augustine struggles with his own life and breaks with his mistress of fifteen years.

Augustine's struggles continue into Book VII. He has largely abandoned Manichaeism, but elements of that thought still compromise his belief that God could become man. His progress away from the dualist vision of Manichaeism forces Augustine to reconsider the question of the source of evil in the world. He concludes that evil must originate from the abuse of free will. It is at this time that Augustine encounters Neoplatonic philosophy. He reads the writings of Plotinus, the father of Neoplatonism, with dedication. Plotinus' reworking of the thought of the pagan philosopher Plato was already considered highly useful by many Church Fathers in the development of Christian thought. In that school of thought Augustine finds a great deal of assistance in grappling with vital issues, including the nature of God, the eternal nature of the soul, and the source of evil. He at the same time finds solace in the Neoplatonist denial of the crucifixion. According to this new way of thinking, man is capable of attaining God through his own efforts. For a time, pride blockaded his further progress. When, however, he takes up the Epistles of Saint Paul, he finds answers that even the Neoplatonists could not provide.

Book VIII witnesses the critical turning point of Augustine's conversion and of the structure of the *Confessions*. Augustine no longer questions the truth but finds his interior will divided. He seeks the advice of Simplicianus, the spiritual father of Ambrose, and hears from him the conversion story of Victorinus, a famous Roman rhetorician. Augustine's struggle continues; he desires conversion but finds himself "weighed down by the pleasant burden of the world" (see *Conf.* VIII.5.12). A fellow countryman from Africa visits him and tells both Augustine and Alypius the story of the conversion of two friends through the reading of a book on the life of Saint Antony. Augustine reaches a crisis between his two wills, the one the expression of habits formed by attachments to the world, the other deeper, more truly free. He famously pleads: "Grant me chastity and self-control, but please not yet" (see *Conf.* VIII.7.17). His rejection of the dualist Manichaeist idea of two natures, "one good, the other evil", is confirmed once again (see *Conf.* VIII.10.22). He sees a vision of Continence and is inspired to take up the writings of Saint Paul, coming immediately upon the verse "Not in dissipation and drunkenness, nor in debauchery and lewdness, nor in arguing and jealousy; but put on the Lord Jesus Christ, and make no provision for the flesh or the gratification of your desires" (VIII.12.29). Months of listening to the preaching and direction of Ambrose finally bear full fruit: Augustine is converted on the spot, to the joy of his mother, Monica.

The last primarily autobiographical portion of the *Confessions* is Book IX. After conversion, Augustine resigns his teaching position and returns to Milan. Augustine, Monica, Augustine's son (Adeodatus), Augustine's brother (Navigius), and five friends leave the city for a long retreat in preparation to receive the sacraments of the Church. He, Adeodatus, and Alypius are baptized at the Easter Vigil of 387. Monica dies during their return trip to Africa, prompting Augustine's grief and reverent remembrance of her holy life.

With Book X, the mode of the *Confessions* shifts from autobiographical narrative to theological exposition. Augustine begins with the question: What is it I love when I love God? He seeks God first in visible creation, and then within his own body and mind. From these failed attempts he turns to the power of memory, the place we look when we seek something that we have lost. This critical consideration of memory is not arbitrary but rather reflects the entire thrust of his autobiographical experiment thus far: reliance upon the instrument of his own memory has brought him to this moment where he can begin to question the larger context of his life (i.e., his—and every man's—relationship with God). In his exploration of memory, Augustine comes to consider the question: How can we seek something unless we already know it; that is, how can we seek God if we don't already know him? After seeking the vestiges of God in memory, however, he concludes that God is not to be found in the mind because God transcends it. As his search for God continues, Augustine acknowledges his continuing struggles against sin. "Nowhere . . . do I find a safe haven for my soul except in you", he prayerfully says to God (see *Conf.* X.40.65).

Moving naturally from the question of memory to the question of that in which memory operates, Book XI addresses the relationship of time to eternity. This leads Augustine to consider the form of God's creation (the "in the beginning" of Genesis) as well as the conception of time in terms of past, present, and future. Since time is always passing away, it leads Augustine to say, "[W]e cannot really say that time exists, except because it tends to non-being" (see *Conf.* XI.14.17). Time appears to be real only in the present. He goes on to consider the problem of measuring time. By the end of the book, he declares that his "thoughts are torn to fragments by tempestuous changes" (see *Conf.* XI.29.39), and turns from his questions in humility to embrace the infinite, unchanging depths of God. Augustine thereby demonstrates clearly that it is only in this embrace of the eternal God that man can transcend the limitations and fluctuations of his own existence in time.

In Book XII, Augustine explores the nature of form and matter, addressing issues central to his personal struggle with Manichaeism. He once again considers particularly the creation account in Genesis, and the challenges philosophy makes to literal biblical exegesis. Augustine examines the whole range of possible interpretations of Genesis and concludes that there is no way to be certain what Moses had in mind when he wrote and that men should take from his words as much of the truth as they are able.

With Book XIII, Augustine returns once again to the opening lines of Genesis. He now considers the agency of the Holy Spirit in creation. He reconsiders questions regarding the importance of words and of language, especially the acts of reading and writing. More keenly aware of the way in which God is present in creation, Augustine begins to reflect on the correspondence between man and the Trinity. Having established these general likenesses between God and himself, the ways in which God is present in his creation while still being beyond it, Augustine now begins to explore his belief that things of creation return to God in ways that are in accord with their nature and capabilities. As man grows in goodness and love, he learns to read, to see things as they are.

Augustine moves toward his conclusion saying it is impossible to see things truly if they are not seen as a gift. To understand the nature of this gift, Augustine distinguishes between gift and fruit. The gift is the thing given. The fruit of the gift, whether in giving or receiving, rests in the spirit in which it is given or received: the fruit is nothing less than a participation in the self-giving that God expressed in the act of creation and that the Spirit continues to express in his ongoing work. If man returns to God, it is because he becomes more like him, freely giving and receiving.

Augustine concludes with a perspective he finds given in Genesis. God, after each of the days of doing his work, calls his work "good". After the completion of all of his work, however, he calls his work "very good"—God beholds the unity of his work, not the sum of its separate days. Seeing this whole is important for Augustine because it is a sign of reading in the Spirit, coming to a unity of vision that he arrives at only through the help of the Spirit. The fundamental weakness of Manichaeism is precisely this failure to grasp this underlying unity.

Having moved beyond the division between the natural man and the spiritual man, beyond a way of seeing that kept the parts of creation from being seen in light of the unitive work of the Spirit, Augustine arrives at a new, more complete understanding of the Sabbath. The Sabbath is not simply a day as man sees it in time. He sees in creation God's order and ministry: the seventh day is an image of the Sabbath, the rest that is promised man in his return to God. He draws a parallel between the creation of the world and the creation of the Church. Man is most like God in giving as God does and in seeing as God does, wholly; those who break God up are separating themselves or only delaying their return. He ends Book XIII with an image of an eternal Sabbath, the final rest in God that is the end of man's journey, the coming to completion of his seeking, knowing, and loving God. The "our heart is unquiet until it rests in you" of the first chapter finds its closure here in an image of an eternal Sabbath at the end.

Words Made Flesh: Summary of
Critical Appraisals and Study Questions

The questions posed in this section are not intended for examination purposes but are designed to prompt appropriate trains of thought for the student to ponder as he reads the work. Questions intended for examination purposes are to be found in the "Study Questions on the Text" at the end of the study guide.

David Vincent Meconi, S.J.: Introduction to the *Confessions*

The heritage of Saint Augustine's *Confessions* is reflected both in the confessional literature that preceded his own and in the myriad of personal memoirs that have followed his example. For Christians in particular, the act of confession was a means for revealing and subjecting their lives more fully to the Word of God. The place of the *Confessions* in the life of the saint is complex, drawing together the influence of his notoriously misspent youth, his connection with Manichaeism, tensions within the Christian hierarchy, and the demands placed by heretical theories upon those who would articulate and promote Christian doctrine. The effect of the work upon its readers reflects Augustine's overall internalization of the phenomenon of allowing his personal life experiences to reveal God's power and agency of grace effectively to Augustine himself and to his readership since.

The *Confessions* should not merely be taken as an autobiography; rather, it must be seen as the narrative of Everyman in his relationship to God. Augustine's aim is not to build up an image of himself through an imposed narrative coherence but rather to reveal the story of the creature in God. For Augustine, intelligibility—of narrative or of existence—is impossible unless human experience is seen in this divine context. Thus God is the principle of coherence, identity, and sanity in the *Confessions*, not the author himself. It is the divine Author and not the human author who is the recurring theme, and through this, Augustine eloquently portrays the particularities of the divine love so long sought by his and every other restless heart.

1. Consider the unconventional opening to Meconi's introduction; what image of Augustine is dramatically conveyed therein? How does this reflect upon your mental image of Augustine? How does it contrast with the images of the Doctor of Grace presented in subsequent critical essays?

2. What was the situation of Valerius, outlined by Meconi, and what was its significance for the elevation of Augustine to the episcopacy and his composition of the *Confessions*? How important is this historical and biographical context to Augustine's position as a saint and as an author?

3. How are memory and time integral to the *Confessions*? What degree of self-awareness (through increased knowledge of God) has been allowed to you through your experience of Augustine's narrative portrayal of these two critical elements?

Allan Fitzgerald, O.S.A.: "Confession, Prayer, Transformation"

The effect of the *Confessions* both upon its author and its readers can most effectively be understood by interpreting the work as a resonating biblical prayer. This interpretation depends upon the encompassing within the notion of confession three elements: professing of faith, confessing of sin, and praising of God. All three of these unite in Augustine to allow him to gain a deeper understanding of himself through confession to God by revealing himself to God and to all. Augustine's achievements are here clearly directed by his embrace of the Scriptures and his incorporation of them into his *Confessions*. His own spiritual journey back to the Church largely involved a slow turning toward the Scriptures and an increased investment in their authority (in place of the texts that had previously directed his attention and opinion). Further, each stage of his journey brought a poignant originality to his developing (and authentically) Christian thought.

With the composition of the *Confessions*, Augustine's self-contextualization of his own life in the framework of the divine economy found narrative voice. The resulting text dramatically reveals Augustine's ongoing dialogue with the incarnate Word. As he matured from a seeker of truth to a Christian, and eventually to an authoritative figure within the Christian community, the reality and personal relevance of scriptural truth became ever more critical to Augustine's growing intimacy with the divine Reality.

1. What, according to Fitzgerald, is the special significance of the Psalms in the fourth century? How is this reflected in Augustine's work?

2. What effect did Manichaeism and Platonism have on Augustine's attitudes toward the Scriptures in particular?

3. What is Fitzgerald's overall assessment of the nature of confession in the *Confessions*? Contrast this with the views provided in the other essays. Are these compatible? Are they equally persuasive or useful in your appreciation of the text?

Joseph T. Lienhard, S.J.: "The *Confessions*: Augustine's First Treatise on Grace"

The theology of grace articulated in the writings of Saint Augustine of Hippo, traditionally called "the Doctor of Grace", was grounded in his personal experience of grace, presented particularly in his

Confessions. In fact, the written recounting of his "conversion story" was possible for Augustine only later in life, after a fuller understanding of the operation of God's grace within his own life. Thus his work is largely illuminated in our understanding when seen through the lens of his reflection on the Epistle to the Romans, composed ten years later and entitled *To Simplicianus: On Various Questions*. Deeply influenced by his interactions with Simplicianus (a priest), Ambrose (the bishop who supervised Augustine's conversion), and the conversion story of Marius Victorinus (an elderly Roman convert), Augustine was brought to revisit and reembrace Saint Paul's Epistles.

This increasingly intimate reacquaintance with Saint Paul brought Augustine to a deeper understanding of the relationship between grace and freedom. This understanding completed his escape from Manichaean materialism and opened the door for his intellectual exploration of the limits of freedom: concupiscence, habit, and original sin. With each passing year, his understanding of the human psyche became ever more complex and nuanced. The operation of grace was not limited to his encounter with Saint Paul, however; it began much earlier with his encounters with Cicero, sacred Scripture, Aristotle, Plotinus, Virgil, and other ancient writers. In his own work he envisioned himself as revisiting the parable of the prodigal son. Through all of this influence and understanding, Augustine's *Confessions* becomes an invitation to his reader: showing forth the action of God's grace in his own life, Augustine reveals the action of God's grace in the life of Everyman.

1. Why does Lienhard say that calling Augustine's 386 decision to be baptized a "conversion" can be misleading? Do you agree?

2. What was the "web of relationships" that developed between Augustine, Ambrose, Simplicianus, and Marius Victorinus? What sort of influence do you think this had on Augustine's spiritual development?

3. What is the "one sentence" from Saint Paul that influenced Augustine so absolutely? Can you discern its influence on the *Confessions*?

4. What are the two sides of Augustine's self-articulation in the role of the prodigal son?

Jared Ortiz: "Creation in the *Confessions*"

Creation is the foundational theme and context for the entirety of Augustine's *Confessions*. His understanding of creation is multifaceted, encompassing the "divine activity" that created everything, the "everything" that God has created, and the essential component for our experience of God himself, eternally defined as Creator, while we, in refracted light, are defined as the created. This necessitates an admission of God's transcendence to the world and to creation itself. Augustine develops the Christian doctrine of creation even further, seeing within it a complex revelation of the Trinity. Consideration of this aspect of Augustine's thought provides an illuminative lens for the structure of the *Confessions* itself.

For Augustine, an integral part of his spiritual journey is bound up in the issue of "coming to terms" with creation, both intellectually and morally. To this end, he must address both the claims of Manichaeism and of Platonism. While the latter provides him with an important intellectual liberation from the false assertions of the former, Augustine must go further. From a proper understanding of creation, Augustine can move on to address the problem of evil, the place of Christ in his theology, the radical effect of the Incarnation on man's relationship with God, the true meaning of confession, and the role and meaning of the Church in the economy of salvation.

1. Articulate the relationship between God and Being. What is the Manichaean error in understanding the relationship between God and his creatures?

2. Explain the *creatio, conversio, formatio* dynamic and its influence on Augustine and on his *Confessions*. How does this explanation of the structure of the book inform your own appreciation of it? Do you agree with Ortiz's assertions?

3. What, according to Ortiz, are the critical elements of Augustine's struggle against Manichaeism? Can you discern these elements in Augustine's writing? What are Docetism and Photinianism, and why did they pose particular challenges to Augustine?

Christopher J. Thompson: "Augustine's *Confessions* and the Source of Christian Character"

Augustine's *Confessions* is the narrative of love from birth to "second birth". Because of its dedicated Christian character, this is not a tale that follows the modern paradigm of self-absorption and introspective angst; on the contrary, it is a work that, by its nature, goes beyond the "self" of its author and gestures toward God, the only thing that can truly satisfy man's restless heart. From this Augustine derives a concrete understanding of the relationship between identity and doctrine, the latter illuminating the former rather than being simply subsumed into it. Against the backdrop of his conversion from Manichaeism, he works to develop an ontology of Christian integrity.

This ontology allows a careful consideration of the human person, the possibility of narrative, and the function of memory while at the same time revealing the centrality of God to discerning or articulating the Christian's story. The understanding of the microlevel of the *Confessions* (i.e., man's experience) is directly reflective of the macrolevel (i.e., the creative order as situated fully within the creative Word). All of this structures the latter portion of Augustine's *Confessions* and likewise provides the proper understanding of the purpose and direction of the preceding and more autobiographical books of the text. Thus the entirety of the *Confessions* demonstrates the centrality of Augustine's christological theology. The chronology of man's experience is fully permeated by the action of God in Christ and his Church. It is through Christ and in him that Augustine, and his reader, learn the true lesson of love.

1. What does Thompson assert is the source of modern frustration with the concluding passages of the *Confessions*? Does this reflect in any way on your own experience of the text?

2. What cosmological implications does Thompson identify in Manichaeism? How are these reflected or combatted in Augustine's writings?

3. What is the significance of the pear theft, according to Thompson? To what degree do you find his Manichaean explanation useful in understanding this famous Augustinian sin?

Things to Think About
While Reading the Book

The questions posed in this section are not intended for examination purposes but are designed to prompt appropriate trains of thought for the student to ponder as he reads the work. Questions intended for examination purposes are to be found in the "Study Questions on the Text" at the end of the study guide.

1. Be attentive to the various meanings and manifestations of "confession" put forth in the *Confessions*. In its original sense, "confession" can mean the confession of personal sin, the profession of faith, and praise of God. What is the relationship between all three? How does Augustine's confession of personal sin enable his profession of faith? What is the difference between the profession of faith and praise of God? What role does confession play in the spiritual life? Who is called to confession throughout the *Confessions*, and how is each confession represented?

2. Manichaeism, founded in the third century, did not merely constitute the major stumbling block to Augustine's conversion; his personal acquaintance with the heresy helped in the development of his own theological understanding. Manichaeism was a dualist religion that claimed to unite a number of wide-ranging religions and even incorporated some superficial elements of Christianity. These elements made Manichaeism particularly seductive to many Christians and even led the Manichaeans to claim to be Christian themselves.

The central tenet of the Manichaean philosophy was dualist, based on a notion of the universe in which a good deity (who commands all things spiritual) and an equally powerful evil deity (who commands all things material) are eternally ranged in a battle against each other. Be attentive to all of the possible effects of this idea: the reduction of evil to an unavoidable characteristic of things material; the glorification of heroic asceticism; the complication of the moral life; etc.

3. In Augustine's combatting of Manichaeism, note the role played by Neoplatonism, the reconsideration of the thought of the philosopher Plato. Consider the influence of Plotinus on Augustine's understanding of the tensions between the material and the spiritual. In what ways is Neoplatonism a stepping-stone to Augustine's eventual conversion? In what ways is it inadequate or a hindrance? Be attentive to the ways in which Neoplatonism is similar to Manichaeism (particularly in terms of the denigration of material reality).

4. The third school of thought that is particularly important to understanding the *Confessions* is Pelagianism, a fifth-century heresy regarding the nature of man and denying original sin as well as the necessity for Christian grace. Pelagianism argues that man has the capacity to seek and attain union with God through his own efforts. Pelagianism was not a primary concern of Augustine at this time (the monk Pelagius was not yet combatting Augustine's theological works), but the seeds of the theory can readily be discerned in emerging notions of human nature. Take note of the way in which Augustine combats this heretical view. How will his understanding of Manichaeism and of Neoplatonism inform his appreciation of this third mode of thought? Further, you may consider the pattern of all of the various philosophical schools considered and explored by Augustine; to what degree is his philosophical engagement with these schools a demonstration of the

evangelical impulse of Christianity? What does this reflect upon the nature of Truth?

5. Augustine's spiritual journey develops from a consideration of the "parts" to an appreciation of the "whole". Watch for the moments where the "whole" is presented as the illuminative lens for these various "parts". Consider the ways in which the *Confessions* should be experienced as a didactic lesson in coming to knowledge of God, and the ways in which its construction reflects Augustine's own coming to such knowledge. In what does knowledge of God consist? You should also be attentive to the role played by education in Augustine's life and in his gradual acceptance of the revelation of Truth.

6. The influence of the *Confessions* on the heritage of confessional and spiritual autobiographical literature has been profound. Scholarly attention, however, has, until the twentieth century, focused more steadily upon Saint Augustine's other writings (particularly the *City of God* and *On the Trinity*). Consider the overarching effect of the *Confessions* on you as a reader. To what degree is it a theological primer, and to what degree is it a spiritually transformative work?

7. Keep in mind the title of Augustine as "Doctor of Grace". What is the place of grace in his autobiographical narrative, and what is its place in his theology? What challenges are placed to grace by the various philosophical schools embraced or combatted by Augustine? What is the relationship between the grace experienced by Augustine and the grace he seeks to convey in his *Confessions*?

Study Questions on the Text of the *Confessions*

Part One—Knowledge of the Text

1. What punishment does Augustine most fear?

2. Which language did Augustine love and which language did he hate in his early education?

3. What was the reaction of Augustine's father when he learned of his son's sexual maturation?

4. What is the subject of Augustine's speech in school?

5. Where does Augustine go away to study briefly in his youth?

6. Against the writings of what classical writer does a young Augustine unfavorably compare sacred Scripture?

7. What particular reassurance does Monica receive that her son (who has then espoused Manichaeism) will repent from his sins and be saved?

8. What does Augustine do in the immediate aftermath of dismissing his mistress (the mother of his illegitimate son) to soothe his grief at her loss?

9. What is the name of the fellow countryman from Africa who visits Augustine in Book XIII?

10. Of what work does this friend speak as an inspiration for conversion?

11. Who is the spiritual father of Ambrose?

12. To what book of the Bible is Augustine's attention drawn in the critical moment of his conversion?

13. What close friend of Augustine converts with him?

14. Where and how does Augustine's mother die?

15. What mental power does Augustine consider in Book X as a bridge between his autobiographical narrative and the more theological exposition yet to come?

Part Two—Essay Questions

1. Consider the many stages of education experienced by Augustine; what does his education illustrate and enable in his life?

2. What is the significance of the Epistles of Saint Paul for Augustine (personally and in the development of his theological understanding)?

3. What is the point of the episode of Augustine's theft of the pears? Why does Augustine himself seek to find the "beauty" of the theft?

4. What in Manichaeism is attractive to Augustine? Are the questions that arise regarding Manichaeism pertinent to a modern audience, and if so, how?

5. Consider Saint Augustine's self-analysis regarding the battle between his conflicting wills (in Book VIII). What does this illustrate with regard to him personally and his understanding of human nature in general?

6. What is the significance of Augustine's struggle with chastity, and what does his struggle with the sins of the flesh bring to his philosophy?

7. What is the nature of evil and what is its place in Augustine's *Confessions* and in his developing theology of grace?

8. Consider Augustine's self-referential use of the parable of the prodigal son (Luke 15:11–32); what does the image of the prodigal signify in and for the *Confessions*?

9. What understanding of sacred Scripture—its role and the means for its proper interpretation—can be gleaned from the *Confessions*?

10. What is the primary genre of the *Confessions*? What is its underlying goal and purpose as a written work, and how is this reflected in its overall structure?

Answer Key for the *Confessions*

Note to Teachers: This answer key can be removed before the study guide is given to the student.

STUDY QUESTIONS

Part One—Knowledge of the Text

1. Being whipped

2. He loved Latin (because it came easily to him) but despised Greek.

3. He anticipated future descendants and joyfully told his wife, Monica.

4. The anger and grief of the goddess Juno

5. Madaura (or Madauros)

6. Cicero

7. She has a dream in which she envisions herself on a wooden rule and is consoled when she is shown that Augustine is standing near her on the same rule.

8. He takes another mistress.

9. Ponticianus

10. The *Life of Antony*

11. Simplicianus, archbishop of Milan

12. Saint Paul's Epistle to the Romans (13:13–14)

13. Alypius

14. Monica dies of fever in Ostia as Augustine and his friends return to Africa. (Note that she dies after her son embraces Christianity.)

15. Memory

Part Two—Essay Questions

1. *Consider the many stages of education experienced by Augustine; what does his education illustrate and enable in his life?*

   Emphasis can be placed here on any moment in Augustine's life: his childhood development, particularly as it was affected by the Christian education by his mother on one hand and the education supervised by his teachers on the other (here Augustine's own attitude regarding the latter should be mentioned); his academic success as a youth (which can be interpreted as both preparing him for later philosophical endeavors and increasing the attraction and the hold of the secular world upon him); his work as a teacher; his personal exploration of various schools of thought; etc. An insightful paper will go further, identifying within this impulse of study a critical indicator of Augustine's "unquiet heart". He seeks understanding that will draw him closer to God and more deeply into loving union with him. More precise observance could also be made of Augustine's maturing attitude toward that which he studies (e.g., the Bible) when considered at various times in his life.

2. *What is the significance of the Epistles of Saint Paul for Augustine (personally and in the development of his theological understanding)?*

This essay should mention the garden scene of Augustine's conversion and his inspired reading of the passage from the Epistle to the Romans. It should also note the preponderance of biblical quotations from the writings of Saint Paul in the latter half of the *Confessions*. From this a number of interesting reflections can be made, including a comparison between Augustine's allusions to other writers or other works (particularly the Psalms), and a consideration of the vital questions to which Saint Paul provided answers in Augustine's quest for Truth. Overall, the essay should demonstrate a consciousness of the themes of the book, not merely a mental registering of the facts of Augustine's life (i.e., it should be shown *why* Saint Paul influenced Augustine so deeply). The critical essays by Fitzgerald and Lienhard will be especially helpful here.

3. *What is the point of the episode of Augustine's theft of the pears? Why does Augustine himself seek to find the "beauty" of the theft?*

First and foremost, the writer of this essay needs to identify the critical point that Augustine's delight was not in the pears but in the act of theft itself. The significance of the fruit itself (both in terms of the sin of Adam and Eve and in terms of Manichaeist ideas concerning fruit) should be addressed at least briefly. Beyond this, a number of interpretive lenses can be effectively applied: the paper can explore elements of free will as well as the degrees and gravity of sin. The critical essay by Thompson will be especially helpful here, though Thompson's theory of the pear theft should not simply be parroted.

4. *What in Manichaeism is attractive to Augustine? Are the questions that arise regarding Manichaeism pertinent to a modern audience, and if so, how?*

At the beginning of the essay, the writer will need to articulate the central philosophy of Manichaeism, explaining its dualistic view of the universe, and briefly state Augustine's relationship to the school of thought. From this, the essay should go on to explore Manichaean doctrine (e.g., Manichaean teachings regarding human nature or the nature of evil) in greater depth, identifying various dangers inherent in it and critically considering the role dualism may play in various modern moral theories. This essay can in a particular way display the reader's appreciation of the enduring relevance of Augustine's work as well as of his life and example. All of the critical essays can be of use here.

5. *Consider Saint Augustine's self-analysis regarding the battle between his conflicting wills (in Book VIII). What does this illustrate with regard to him personally and his understanding of human nature in general?*

   Augustine's relationship to Manichaeism can be mentioned with particular effect here. It should be shown how Augustine's theory of conflicting wills is similar to or different from Manichaeist dualism and its treatment of human nature. The role of the human will in sin can be addressed. This essay can address many of the same issues that would arise in an essay responding to the next question (regarding chastity), but it should at the same time clearly demonstrate comprehension of the significance of Augustine's consideration of the human will in the context of his understanding of moral law and of man's relationship with God. Free will, in particular, should be addressed.

6. *What is the significance of Augustine's struggle with chastity, and what does his struggle with the sins of the flesh bring to his philosophy?*

   Once again, the writer of this essay should have effective recourse to a consideration of Manichaeism and its notion of the spiritual and the material being eternally in conflict. This essay should demonstrate an understanding of sin (and various theories of the nature of evil), questions regarding the human will, and the nature of both concupiscence and personal culpability in sin. Various autobiographical elements can be usefully considered here as well, including Augustine's opinion regarding childhood innocence, the cultural importance placed on fathering sons (captured both in the enthusiasm of Augustine's father at his own son's sexual maturation and the joy of Augustine himself at the birth of even an illegitimate son), Saint Paul's writings concerning temptation and the sins of the flesh, the barrier that the sins of the flesh presented to Augustine's progress toward conversion (this is perhaps the most obvious element to consider), or a comparison with the recurring sin of Alypius with regard to gladiatorial games. The writer may even theorize regarding the effect of the sins of the flesh on a man gifted with a brilliant philosophical mind.

7. *What is the nature of evil and what is its place in Augustine's* Confessions *and in his developing theology of grace?*

   Like many of the other essay questions, this question should inspire the writer to consider various doctrines concerning human nature. It should (like question 5) require a careful delving into questions regarding free will and sin. To what degree does a particular understanding of the nature of evil illuminate our understanding of man and of God? The conflicting accounts of evil provided in the *Confessions* should be at least briefly outlined (particularly Manichaeism contrasted with Christianity; the superior essay will not neglect Neoplatonism either). All of the critical essays will be useful here.

8. *Consider Augustine's self-referential use of the parable of the prodigal son (Luke 15:11–32); what does the image of the prodigal signify in and for the* Confessions?

   This essay must identify passages of the *Confessions* in which Augustine clearly aligns himself with the prodigal of the Gospel. Further, however, it should explore the nature of Everyman's relationship with God the Father in terms of prodigality: the nature of sin, but also the nature of grace. This essay can explore the subject in the light of Augustine's consideration of God the Creator or can study the structural trajectory of the work from prodigality to faith or can consider the prayerful intercessory role of Monica in her son's conversion. Overall, however, it needs to demonstrate an understanding of grace and of the enduring love that God generously bestows upon his creatures.

9. *What understanding of sacred Scripture—its role and the means for its proper interpretation—can be gleaned from the* Confessions?

The writer of this essay cannot simply parrot Augustine's treatment of this question in the light of Manichaeist tensions (pitting the literal against the figurative), though these should be thoughtfully outlined from the beginning. This essay should go further in exploring the significance of the question of interpretation and the pressing relevance of sacred Scripture to every man. (Questions of biblical exegesis proper to the Protestant Reformation could be referenced, but a clear understanding of historical chronology would need to be shown at the same time.) The particular importance of the Bible in the life of Augustine should also be noted (particularly the Psalms and the writings of Saint Paul).

10. *What is the primary genre of the* Confessions? *What is its underlying goal and purpose as a written work, and how is this reflected in its overall structure?*

This essay should address a wide range of issues considered in response to the preceding essay questions, particularly the various meanings of "confession" that are represented in the text. It should consider the place of Augustine's autobiographical account in the history of literature as well as his role as narrator. Further, it must take into consideration the work's form as a dialogue between Augustine and God, and the way in which the work functions as the story of "Everyman" in relationship to God. A basic knowledge of the heritage of spiritual autobiography (provided at least in passing in most of the critical essays) should be shown. Meconi's introduction to the *Confessions* will prove especially useful here.